Flight of Honey

I0092914

Poems by Dianne Borsenik

LUCHADOR PRESS

Luchador Press
Big Tuna, TX

Copyright © Dianne Borsenik, 2023
First edition 1 3 5 7 9 10 8 6 4 2
ISBN: 978-1-958182-39-0
LCCN: 2023937321

Author photo: James Borsenik
Title page image: Dianne Borsenik
Cover image: Marcy and Doug Ritzert

"In poet Dianne Borsenik's new book *Flight of Honey,* the sounds of music, homages to visual art, maps of family geography, interactions with nature, and married life and related concerns, combine in a poetry collection that is as satisfying, fluid, and sticky as the titular sweetener. If ever a writer deserved to be Poet Laureate of Ohio, it would be Dianne Borsenik."

—Gregg Shapiro, author of *Refrain in Light* (Souvenir Spoon Press, 2023)

"Borsenik's new collection of poems is a lyrical journey through a year of experiences that mirror the changing seasons. In free verse poems, haiku, and haibun, Borsenik explores the tensions of life's highs and lows. One moment we can relish a "golden weekend" with days like honey, "richly aureate," and the next, we hunker down, struggle amid the booms and busts of history. Through it all, there is plenty of music, a soundtrack in language and in images— from a grandfather strumming a dulcimer somewhere in a West Virginia hollow to Aretha Franklin belting out her classic "Respect," to the music of the universe, "one giant composition plucked out / on a cosmic guitar."

—Chuck Salmons, author of *Patch Job* (Night Ballet Press, 2017) and *Stargazer Suite* (11thour Press, 2016)

"In this sweet collection, spiked with the poet's desire to live longer than her mother did ("genetic advantage/is not in my charts,") we have zany moments where Jesus roams the Walmart parking lot, sixties lyrics zing, and birds and feral cats screech in Midwest intersections. But the poems revel also in serious seasons of honey tasting, including the latter days, "the best of all," as Borsenik fills her hive with finely realized echo puns, ekphrasis, haiku, haibun, and many free-verse form explorations. We usually say this about fiction, but I have to say about this book of poems: I couldn't put it down."

—Diane Kendig, author of *Woman With a Fan:
On Maria Blanchard* (Shanti Arts, 2021)

"For something so sweet, honey has a surprising depth of flavor, secret floral notes buried under waves of fructose and glucose. Similarly, the poetry of Dianne Borsenik will surprise you if you let it. There is joy and tranquility here that sometimes bubbles with mad effervescence, but also darker currents as she explores rustbelt landscapes, the Appalachian diaspora, the daughter-of-a-daughter-inlaw's blues, and her own mortality. Like the "flight of honey" in her title poem, she follows the seasons, tasting deep and mixing poetic forms to find her buried treasures. You will find haibun, ekphrastic poems, words on the wings of an uknown bird, and Jesus traipsing into Walmart. Much to loveand wonder over!"

—R. C. Wilson, editor/publisher of Last Exit Press,
curator of Last Exit Open Poetry Readings in Kent, OH

Acknowledgments:

"Heat" — *Gasconade Presents: Wolf at the Door, Nobody Home* (2023), "Ice Cubes" — *Nother Ring Round the Jawbone* (2022), *Gasconade Presents: Wolf at the Door, Nobody Home* (2023), "In the Thick of It" — *Pudding Magazine* (2023), "I Tell James Not to Hit Jesus as We Circle the Walmart Parking Lot on Halloween" — *Chiron Review* (2020), "Loud Enough to Wake the Dead" — *Birds of the Cuyahoga* (Edith Chase Symposium, 2022), "Up the Mountain" — *Slipstream* (2022), featured in *Lit Cleveland's Humanities Festival* (2022), "What You Need" — *Gasconade Presents: Wolf at the Door, Nobody Home* (2023), *Best of Ohio Poetry Anthology* (2021, 2nd place, Music category), "We Could Do Worse" — *Songs for Wild Ohio* - 2023 Edith Chase Symposium anthology (Last Exit Press, 2023) "Kettle" — *Songs for Wild Ohio* - 2023 Edith Chase Symposium anthology (Last Exit Press, 2023)

Many thanks to Anna Batyreva of Happy Bear Honey, LLC, for her insights on beekeeping and honey.

Much gratitude to Jason Ryberg for making this book possible.

Author's Note:

The poem *The Unspooling of Spring* is a reverse abecedarian. The lines start with the first thirteen letters of the alphabet and end, in reverse order, with the last thirteen letters. This may not be obvious with the margins constraining the form. The forward slashes indicate full lines.

TABLE OF CONTENTS

Author's Biography
haiku bio: silver-haired woman

For my husband James, who has always been
the honey in my life

"Honey tasting is like wine tasting—
you wait for the bouquet and flavors
to cascade over you."

—Claire Jones, "A Taste of Honey,"
from Keeping Backyard Bees.com

Ice Cubes

Friends are ice cubes in the cocktail of life.
We chill together, tinkle and clink our way

out of the shaker and into the glass, mix
with sass and effervescence, irreverence

and unabashed joy; we entertain one long-
pour, united in spirit, no matter the garnish.

Crush us, we stay frosty; swizzle-stir us, we
go with the flow. We get juicy; we get saucy—

we get what it means to melt together
as we age, diluting the bad times, enhancing

the good times, with just enough bump
and tumble to let them know we were here.

Friends are ice cubes in the cocktail of life.
This is our celebration. This is our Happy Hour.

Sui Generis

—after the photograph "Undulating" by Betsy Parker

You can almost hear the music—not guitar
or piano or flute, nothing so conventional—no,

it would require dulcimer,
balalaika, tongue drum or didgeridoo

to produce the rhythmic undulations
of this exotic dance. The occupation of space,

the sturdiness of limb, emotion behind the motion,
everything's in place. You can almost hear her laughter

at the shifting play of sunlight on her bare skin,
feel her jubilation at the timelessness of her art.

Sisters surround on this arboreal stage, content
to gently leaf and be. But she, sui generis, says

Why conform when you're born to stand out?
Keep on corkscrewing toward the stars.

The Unspooling of Spring
—after Van Gogh's "Starry Night"

Ad astra—to the stars, to those chips of mica and capiz, / because earthly sky is too ordinary for spring. Body / cannot frolic within the confines of cloud and solar lux. /

Dance demands space for maneuvering, for fling, for flow, / expression unrestrained—deliberate, but open to improv. /

Forget everything you've been taught; the form of haiku / gambols and wins its case, both classic and current. /

Heretofore, the witchery of bare feet and wet grass; / in its stead, the unspooling of celestial zephyr, / joyous, undeniable, a grand cosmic torque. /

Keeping the faith means transcending worship, / leaving antiquated mythology in terrestrial dust. *Con brio* / means achieving escape velocity, means becoming reborn.

Up the Mountain
—Gauley Bridge, Fayette County, West Virginia

Grandfather never spoke a word to me
that I can remember, never held me
on his lap, never smiled in my presence,
didn't hold hands, didn't hug. I was his eldest
grandchild, but not beloved. He never
took me up the mountain with my dad
to inspect the garden, although I begged.
Bears, he'd mutter, and *Copperheads.*
They never took a gun or knife with them
for protection during this unwavering ritual,
and they never returned with vegetables.
What was up the mountain, I now wonder,
a backdoor woman to visit, or a copper still?
With both of them gone, I'll never know.

*

Grandmother mocked my Ohio accent;
this one's a Northerner, she would
say to friends or relatives we'd encounter,
repeating *"I-eee, I-eee"* as if I
were a surprise visitor from another
country, strange and incomprehensible.
I was her eldest grandchild, but no favorite
in her eyes. *You look too much like me,*
my mother explained, without going
into details about the estrangement
between them. Grandmother ignored me as
she floured her homemade biscuits, worked
her loom. She never shared stories about
my dad's childhood, never asked about mine.

*

Without fail, as premature dusk began
to smother mountain hollows,
Grandfather produced his mountain dulcimer,
not asking who wanted to listen, assuming
we would welcome his nightly entertainment
in this place bereft of television, radio,

close-by neighbors. His arthritic hands
rollicked over the frets, strummed strings
without complaint, brought forth a concert
that would not have been out of place
two hundred, three hundred years ago.

Blood doesn't always call to blood.
If ever I think about my grandparents,
it's the mountain's music I miss most of all.

The Flowering

"You are endangering the whole world.
Stop firing at the nuclear...facility! Immediately stop firing!"
—unnamed worker, Zaporizhzhia, Ukraine

No one mentioned
the invention of the wheel
or the origin of sliced bread.
No one said a word
about dice or the role
chance played in the deal.
It's all just taken for granted,
the luminous mysteries
of gas-driven engines
and harnessed electricity,
of air-conditioning,
microwaves, and computers
the size of a wristwatch.
No one mentioned the
sorrowful mysteries of
a chain reaction, fission,
plutonium-239, the punching
of a set of numbers, of madmen
determined to end it all.

Thunderstruck

Crack of wood, thud of heaviness, air displaced. House shudders. Tulip tree next door has crashed into the street, taking tangled wires with it. Sharp gusts continue. House trembles. Internet is dark, room is dark, sky is dark. Bombardment of rain begins.

striking hard enough
to leave a mark
first day of spring

massive construction
next to the funeral home
noise to raise the dead

yesterday's 60s
but a memory
—the chill of time

What You Need
—after Aretha Franklin's "Respect"

What you need, do you know I got it?
1967, a small white transistor radio.

It's the Summer of Love, baby, but
Detroit burns, Ginsberg chants to levitate
the Pentagon, Joan Baez blocks the entrance
to Oakland's Armed Services Induction Center,
John McCain is shot down and becomes a P.O.W.
Protests against the war in Vietnam
surge; troops engage in the Mekong Delta.
All they're *askin' is for a little respect*
when they come home.

Far out, man, *Hair* opens off-Broadway,
Hendrix wants to know if you've
ever been Experienced, Morrison is
getting high(er). *Sock it to me,*
Sock it to me, Sock it to me, Sock it to me....
The Queen of Soul climbs the charts.

What you want, baby I got it.
Martin Luther King is jailed for peaceful
protest, Carl Stokes is elected mayor
of Cleveland, President Johnson appoints
Thurgood Marshall as Supreme Court Justice.
Take care, T. C. B.
The Freedom of Information Act
becomes effective, the Outer Space Treaty
is signed. It's a Human Be-In,
a magical mystery tour through a Cold War,
a Space Race, the Motown Sound at CKLW
coming to you out of Windsor-Detroit.

It's the 60s, baby, a transistor radio,
a twelve-year old girl listening to a Queen.
Find out what it means to me.
Aretha, nothing but *R-E-S-P-E-C-T.*

pollen dust
    everywhere
spring's fingerprints

The Golden Weekend

April, unseasonably warm. Riding in the convertible, top down, first pink of the year on skin that hasn't seen the sun in over five months. Two days of eighty degrees Fahrenheit, no rain, a golden weekend. By Wednesday, lake effect snow is predicted. *That's Ohio,* they say. *If you don't like the weather, wait a minute.*

bare branches
trembling
      at the touch
of spring tease

Loud Enough to Wake the Dead

"Birds are the only dinosaurs...still alive today."
—*Michael Lee, evolutionary biologist*

"If history repeats itself, I am so getting a dinosaur."
—*Anonymous*

A bright piece of sky swoops
down and screams at me
loud enough to wake the dead.
I nearly jump out of my skin
before I process he's the first
of a party arriving for lunch.
The daily scattering of peanuts
on the front porch offers
a standing reservation. One
after another the jays screech
in, alighting on the railing
for a momentary grace
before snatch and escape.

It's easy enough to imagine
them as pint-sized raptors
evolved to be keen of eye

and broad of wing, bold
and resourceful. I don't know
if I'll ever get used to the idea
of T-Rex stomping around
like a giant rooster, feathers
flying as he screams and pecks
at the other pre-avians.

I want dinosaurs to be
like the ones in my 1960s
How and Why Wonder Book,
like the Winking Lizard iguana,
but those depictions seem
to have met with irrefutable
revision. It's hard to change,
to let go of things, when
perceptions embed so deeply.
At least I can depend on my
own little sky-blue band of
dinosaurs to return tomorrow,
insatiable and peanut-crazy,
piping, jeering, screaming
loud enough to wake the dead.

Flight of Honey

"Gathered in the sleepy orchards of
Lorain County, Ohio" —Happy Bear Honey LLC

1.
Anna says *It's sweeter*
at the beginning of the season,
when the bees have just begun
to gather their nectar from
honey locust and clover,
all the wildflowers of equinox
and Beltane, sleepy orchards
awakening to the year.

> *clusters dissolve into*
> *hymn of new leaves*
> *and filtered sunlight*

—*a timeless confection*
  caught in pale amber—

2.
Solstice, Midsummer, Mead
Moon. Linden's snowy ambrosia
sirens a sophisticated dance

to its brief blossoms. Longest
days provide abundant pollen
for the developing brood.

—allow the inspiration of wood
and menthol before the savoring
of moonglitter mint—

wings fanning the cells

3.
Estival scorch, and beanstalk
fireweed quilts the meadow,
every spike a fuse. The nectar,
a wartime translation. Bees carry
mouthfuls of candy bombs
back to hungry hives.

—a flute of creamy champagne
explodes on the tongue—

hum building
inside the honeycombs . . .
plant dahlias, poppies, oregano
to ease the dearth

4.
Mabon transubstantiates sunbeams—
slanted low through varicolored
foliage—into goldenrod, each
inflorescence gravid with bees.
Time grows short to build the cache;
unsettled weather looms.

—dark shimmer of liquid topaz
  maple syrup with a bit of bite
  buttery before swallowing—

        drones ejected
        bounty reserved
        to sustain the colony

5.
Anna says . . . *Butterscotch.*
Hunter's Moon appears
above weeks-long fade to brown,
but earth has kept a secret trove
to slake the needs of bees.
What sources beguile, mysterious?
Anna says *I really wish I knew*
because I'd plant more of them.

before the long shiver of winter
this final perfect yield

—distinctive, robust, finesse
of caramel and brown sugar
a special surprise, the color

like these days,
richly aureate—
the best of all.

Kettle

*—Intersection of Electric Blvd.
and Parsons Dr., Avon Lake, Ohio*

First, the kettle:
  a grand stir of blue
    by swooping black
      feathers catching
        the late afternoon
          sun. Everyone stops
            to stare at the sight
              of so many. Then
                realization, oak filled
                  with a hundred, large
                  as eagles, roosting.

What kind of bird is that?

One woman asks.
I don't know; I've
never see this before.
*Must be some kind
of hawk,* I answer,

unaware that later
research fails to
identify. It's okay—
some glories
should remain
unexplained.

Good Vibrations

—after Jo Ann Buzulencia's photograph
"Swimming in Blue"

"If you want to find the secrets of the universe,
think in terms of … vibration."—Nikola Tesla

It's vibration, man, always was, still is.
We are one giant composition plucked out
on a cosmic guitar, each string vibrating
at its own frequency, energy unceasing,

and when the bits come together we
sync up, fireflies flashing at the same time,
the Beach Boys grooved to it in '66,
good vibrations, they knew the score.

The following year, the Beatles turned on—
I am he…as you are me and we are
all together, each of us alone but connected,
swimming laps in this crystal blue pool of

consciousness. Dig it—the inherent blueness
of water is the only known example
of a natural color caused by vibrational
conversion, it doesn't get more real than
that, the music of the spheres made flesh,
repetition, modulation, improvisation,
everything and everyone a kind of intrinsic blue,
shifting patterns chasing the perfect chord.

If You Are the Queen of England, Drones Will Form the Shape of a Corgi in the Sky*

and if you're not, you must welcome
a more pedestrian extravaganza.

Pyrotechnic chrysanthemums will
flare and shower their way across

your celebration, Roman candles
will jubilee with whistle and bang.

No Trooping the Colour, no balcony
appearances for commoners—but you

never thought of yourself as *common,*
did you? Common, meaning ordinary,

meaning familiar, everyday. Not royal.
Lack of crown never slowed your bold

design. You know you love exuberance;
you know you'll find your place among

the luminaries. On this velvety stage
of life, you know you're a star.

*—after Lynne Provance's stained glass
art piece "Bursting Extravaganza"
and the Queen's Platinum Jubilee, 2022

My Husband Goes Out to Feed the Birds and Has an Otherworldly Experience

at least that's what I thought for one hot minute
this morning. I heard him saying *Git! Go on, git!*
so when he came inside I asked him what he was
shooing away and he said "the grays" and the
first picture that came to mind was him vamoosing
big-headed, wide-eyed aliens out of the front yard
instead of stray neighborhood cats. I don't know
why the scientists at the Oak Ridge National
Laboratory in Tennessee are experimenting to find
a portal to a parallel universe when this dimension
is strange enough. I mean, I don't think anyone in
the world would overreact if an alien spacecraft
landed in downtown Cleveland, or anywhere, really,
because we've lived through a global pandemic, a
surreal insurrection, some badass weather-related
events, and a shortage of chicken wings, all just in
the past couple of years. About the only thing that
scares me now is an asthma attack.

go on! git,
little four-legs—I'm allergic
to death

In the Thick of It

*"What's fire smell like? ...Oh, fire can smell delightful...
depending on the logs, that's a great smell."*
—*Jeff Goldblum,* The Late Show with Stephen Colbert

We're in the thick of it now,
the smoke of this century,
this decade, this year, this month,
this week, this day. It has been
smoldering beneath the mountain,
deep within the veins of coal,
undetected and unaddressed,
for longer than we can imagine
and now it's out of control.
No longer a backyard fire pit
or cozy campground bonfire,
no boutique candle in the dark,
these flames are wild and dangerous.
There's no escaping the heat
and there's no ignoring its advance.
None of us are getting any younger.

We're in the thick of it now—
there's nothing left for us to do
but breathe in, breathe out
the scorched timber of our lives,
pine and cedar, incense.

Focus

—Elyria, Ohio, located
at the forks of the Black River,
23 miles southwest of Cleveland

Elyria was a boom town back when
I was a kid. The county's factories
offered steady paychecks—with overtime—
to the Appalachian diaspora fleeing
the crushing poverty of the hills.
Entire families uprooted to resettle "up north,"
bringing brothers and uncles and cousins
with them to fill the floors of American Standard,
Ford Assembly, the US Steel plant.
All the stay-at-home mothers shopped
downtown, where Loomis' giant camera sign
flashed its giant lightbulb. We kids
were convinced it was taking our photos;
we always made faces at it.

*

Midway Mall killed the downtown in 1967—
and now it too stands dead and derelict.
All the major factories went bankrupt
or moved away, scraping the county
into the dustpan of the Rust Belt.
Cascade Park's sledding hill, where
generations of Elyrians picnicked
and watched fireworks every Fourth of July,
has been renovated into a broad road
sweeping down to a basin of spindly new trees.
Weeds fill the parking lots of restaurants;
empty hotels litter the landscape.
The giant camera is long gone.

*

Black River, with its twin cascades, still
twists, tumbles, and flows through the heart
of Elyria, just as it did in 1817 when Heman Ely
founded the city. Loomis' giant camera sign
has turned up in a Cincinnati museum;
I'm sure kids still make faces at it. If only

it really had worked and captured the boom
before the bust. Before ghosted alleyways,
collapsed hopes, and the dissipation of *better*.
We kids who chose to stay—lucky enough
to have found jobs and kept homes—
now drive through Elyria's pot-holed,
siren-streaked streets, past the gap-toothed
grimace of downtown, picking our way
through the bones of a once-mighty behemoth.

Wasted

Living
plants already
there torn out to make room
for a memorial garden…
of plants.

Resurrection

October, unseasonably warm. Riding home in the convertible, top down. Too many days of post-op hospitalization, difficult, stifling. The light is benediction. Dazed by medication. Passing houses like passing minutes, one smoothed into another. Squint against the sun. The light is communion. Could have died without surgery. Time passes, borrowed time. The light is epiphany.

in the rearview
baskets of summer annuals
discarded curbside

I Tell James Not to Hit Jesus as We Circle the Walmart Parking Lot on Halloween

He's the Baptist version of Jesus: a young,
white male with long, curly, nut-brown hair
and a bushy beard, wearing a white robe with
a knotted cord around His waist. Instead of
sandals, He has on what appear to be black
work boots, but that makes sense, in Ohio,
in October, in the rain.

I begin to wonder what Jesus needs so badly
on an early Halloween afternoon. He's clearly
already dressed for any event He might plan
to attend. He might be after some kind of food
or beverage contribution for a party, or maybe
He's decided, at the last minute, to pass out
candy to trick-or-treaters.

I imagine He finds Walmart a little cheaper
than Heaven, where you have to pay for your
sins with blood. Here, in Walmart, there's just

about anything you want for pennies on the
dollar, shiny, new, made in China, or Mexico,
or in the States, untainted by guilt or sacrifice,
self-checkout available.

We Could Do Worse

—for James, Cleveland Metroparks Rocky River Reservation, Ohio

Scuffing through butterscotch and candied-apple,
chartreuse and pumpkin and tangerine,
macadam path a tattered carpet of crunch,
he engulfs my hand with his as we inhale autumn,
each breath warm honey and mulled wine.

Prehistoric Dunkleosteus—a monstrous fish, fanged
and armored sovereign of its Late Devonian
food chain—scythed the waters that once sculpted
the basin of floodplain forest where we walk.

Fossilized remains, excavated cliffside in this
Reservation, evolved into the intimidating replica
displayed in the Nature Center. Children angle
for photos next to its gaping jaws.

We could do worse than die, here, now,
bequeathing our bones to deep time, facsimiles
pressed into some far-distant version of Ohio Shale.

We could do worse than defy the extinction
of our species, be exhibited as the last of our kind.

Look, some awed future alien intelligence might
murmur, *Look at how they perished together—*
Look at how the bodies touch.
Look, they might wonder, *They moved in pairs.*

Heat

he turns up the heat

she turns down the heat
caught in the middle

blankets folded back, waiting
for the slide in of cold feet
the snuggle, the settle, sleep

I Tell James Not to Hit Santa Claus
Riding His Bicycle on New Year's Eve

He's the grunge version of Santa, flannelled
and grim faced, clearly not in the holiday spirit.
It's a week after Christmas and his mission is
finished, but he must have exhausted all his jolly
delivering the goods because he's having none of
        it now.

It's disappointing to see him out of uniform—
without sleigh or reindeer, without the Mrs. and the
elves, nary a cookie in sight—navigating side roads
in the dusk and drizzle. He must feel discarded, now
the exaltation has expired and the focus is on a
soon-to-be-newborn year.

Did he cross against traffic to mock the status quo?
Why should he be responsible for the whole of it—
the material fulfillment, promises of love, a season
of peace, stacked odds of a white Christmas—for

such a brusque reward? It's no wonder he'd rebel,
pedal off into obscurity for another eleven months,
against the light, against the odds, against the world.

advisory—heavy fog
moving into
the New Year

Lunar New Year
hops in, furs the trees
with white

Fairytale

Every single branch is spray-painted silver with a thick coating of ice. The low afternoon sun makes the trees appear to be lit from within. Along this enchanted shore of Lake Erie is a fairytale world of no pandemic, no war, no worries. It's a snow globe, a bubble in time. I want to look everywhere at once. I don't want to look away.

frosting on the cake—
sharing this
      with him

Knotted Together

My birthday arrives with just enough bluster
and fuss to tell me the universe is still amused

that I was born. Never the easy road,
the dinner reservation that goes without a hitch.

This evening forecasts historic snow, a glaze
of ice to arrive sometime around the hour

we'll be getting home. We're determined to go.
Some years the carrot, some years the stick,

always the push forward toward living longer
than my mother did. Genetic advantage

is not in my charts. I find myself at the window,
watching our usual knot of sparrows mobbing

the feeders, bits of chestnut life beating the air,
never still, always hungry. A suspect shadow

or breath of sound and they scatter like mad,
leafing the bare branches of the wisteria

and lilac. They always return *en masse,* pecking
each other to get at the good stuff. Today

is my birthday, one more year marking a flock
of years that seem both impossibly scattered

and unbelievably knotted together, another
year returning, still hungry for the good stuff.

Dianne Borsenik is active in the northern and mid-Ohio poetry communities. Recent work has appeared in *I Thought I Heard a Cardinal Sing: Ohio's Appalachian Voices* (Sheila-Na-Gig Editions, 2022), *Ashes to Stardust: A David Bowie Tribute Anthology* (Sybaritic Press, 2023), *Slipstream, Pudding Magazine,* and *Songs of Wild Ohio* (Edith Chase Symposium, Last Exit Press, 2023). Poems are forthcoming in *Gasconade Review: Wolf at the Door, Nobody Home* and *Of Rust and Glass - Roots.* In 2023, *Raga for What Comes Next* (Stubborn Mule Press, 2019), a full-length collection of Borsenik's poems, was featured in the Modern and Contemporary American Poetry course at Muskingum University. Actor

Jonathan Frid used three of her poems in his one-man show *Genesis of Evil,* Speak of the Devil (Lorain, Ohio) named a cocktail after her, and Lit Youngstown printed her poem "Disco" on their tee shirts, which makes her feel like a rock star. Borsenik lives in Elyria, Ohio, with her husband James. Find her on Facebook and at www.dianneborsenik.com.

"Often, I begin to write a straightforward poem and some fanciful head trip takes over — a walk in the park invokes dinosaurs, a ride in the car discovers Santa Claus. I've learned to groove in whatever direction the poem wants to go."

silver-haired woman—
   lifelong flowerchild poet
    writing her raga